COUNTDOWN TO SPACE

HUBBLE SPACE TELESCOPE
Exploring the Universe

Michael D. Cole

Series Advisor:
John E. McLeaish
Chief, Public Information Office, retired,
NASA Johnson Space Center

Library of Congress Cataloging-in-Publication Data

Cole, Michael D.
     Hubble Space Telescope : exploring the Universe / Michael D. Cole.
          p.   cm. — (Countdown to space)
     Includes bibliographical references and index.
     Summary: Details the initiation of the Hubble Space Telescope in April 1990
and the repair and servicing missions that followed; explains the telescope's role
in answering questions about the universe.
     ISBN: 0-7660-1120-8
     1. Hubble Space Telescope (Spacecraft)—Juvenile literature. 2. Astronomy—
Research—Juvenile literature. 3. Astronautics in astronomy—Juvenile literature.
[1. Hubble Space Telescope (Spacecraft) 2. Astronomy. 3. Astronautics.]
I. Title. II. Series.
QB500.268.C65   1999
522'.2919—dc21   98-3298
                                                                CIP
                                                                 AC

Printed in the United States of America

10 9 8 7 6 5 4 3 2

Illustration Credits: National Aeronautics and Space Administration
(NASA), pp. 7, 9, 11, 13, 17, 18, 21, 23, 25, 27, 40; NASA/STScI, pp. 4, 31,
38; NASA/STScI/AURA, pp. 33, 36, 37, 39; S. Terebey (Extrasolar Research
Corp.) and NASA, p. 41.

Cover Illustration: NASA (foreground); Raghvendra Sahai and John Trauger
(JPL), the WFPC2 science team, NASA, and AURA/STScI (background).

*Cover photo: The robotic arm has a firm hold on the Hubble Telescope in the
payload bay of the space shuttle.*

CONTENTS

The Hubble Space Telescope sits in the payload bay of the space shuttle.

1

A Telescope Bound for Space

The Hubble Space Telescope was carefully loaded into the payload bay of the space shuttle *Discovery*. Astronomers, engineers, and other scientists had spent fifteen years designing and building the mighty telescope. Finally, it was ready for its journey into space. In the middle of April 1990, *Discovery* and its long-awaited cargo rolled slowly to the launchpad at Cape Canaveral, Florida.

The giant telescope had cost more than $1.6 billion! Scientists had faced many problems in constructing the telescope. Most of them believed their years of difficult effort were worth it. If the telescope worked, it would be the most powerful telescope ever built.

Finally, the day for which these scientists had long

been waiting had arrived. *Discovery* sat on the launchpad with the Hubble Space Telescope inside, ready for its historic ride into space.

As the countdown continued, those who had worked on the telescope watched and listened. If all went well, *Discovery*'s crew of astronauts would release the telescope into orbit the following day. Strapped to their seats, the astronauts listened to the countdown on their helmet headsets.

T minus one minute and counting . . .

Like the thousands of people who had worked on the telescope, the astronauts braced themselves for the approaching moment of liftoff.

The final seconds ticked down.

Five . . . four . . . three . . . two . . . one . . .

Orange fire and huge clouds of smoke gushed outward from the space shuttle *Discovery*'s engines. The tremendous thrust lifted the shuttle off the pad.

" . . . And liftoff of the space shuttle *Discovery*," the NASA announcer said, "with the Hubble Space Telescope—our window on the universe."[1]

Discovery roared through the sky toward space. As it climbed higher and higher, the solid rocket boosters and the external fuel tank separated from the shuttle. Minutes later the shuttle was in orbit.

The next day, *Discovery*'s crew opened the payload bay doors. The Hubble Space Telescope, named after

American astronomer Edwin Hubble, was then released into orbit around Earth.

It was more than three weeks before the telescope's instruments were ready to look at their first object in space. After all the waiting, astronomers had high hopes for this amazing machine.

Astronomers had long wanted a telescope in space. The biggest reason for such a telescope was simple: All light from space that reaches a telescope on the ground is blurred by Earth's atmosphere. A telescope in space, above Earth's atmosphere, would be able to see objects in space much more clearly. Without the blurring effect

The space shuttle Discovery *lifts off, carrying a crew of five and the Hubble Space Telescope.*

of Earth's atmosphere, it would also be able to see much farther out into space.

The most important part of the Hubble Space Telescope was an eight-foot-wide mirror. This primary mirror was designed to focus on distant objects in the universe like never before. Light from a distant star or galaxy would reflect off this large mirror and onto a series of smaller mirrors, bouncing the light into what was called the Wide Field Planetary Camera, or WF/PC. Because of this abbreviation, everyone called the camera the "wiff pic."[2]

The WF/PC records the object's image and stores it in a computer. The computer then relays the image to the Space Telescope Science Institute in Baltimore, Maryland, where a team of astronomers studies it.

Many highly complex scientific instruments for measuring the mirror's reflected light were placed aboard the Hubble Space Telescope. The Faint-Object Camera was designed to take pictures of dim objects in space that can barely be seen from Earth. The Faint-Object Spectrograph would examine the different colors of light coming from these objects. By this method, scientists could learn the object's temperature, as well as its chemical and gas makeup.[3] The Goddard High-Resolution Spectrograph would look at objects in space, focusing on a special kind of radiation called ultraviolet light. Ultraviolet light is invisible to human eyes. The Hubble Space Telescope would give scientists a great new opportunity to observe this type of light from space.[4] The brightness of light coming from a star or galaxy would be measured by the High-Speed Photometer. This measurement would help astronomers learn about the size of the object in space, as well as its distance from Earth.

While the Hubble Space Telescope *is* a telescope, it is also a spacecraft. It is powered by a set of solar arrays attached to either side of the telescope. Its guidance system is used to point the telescope in the direction of the object scientists wish to view. This system is very important. The many powerful instruments aboard the Hubble would be useless if scientists were unable to aim and focus the telescope effectively.

By May 20, 1990, the Hubble Space Telescope was ready to be aimed at its first target in space. The engineers, astronomers, and other scientists involved with the project believed the telescope's systems were ready for operation. Hundreds of these scientists gathered in control rooms at the Goddard Space Flight Center in Greenbelt, Maryland, the Marshall

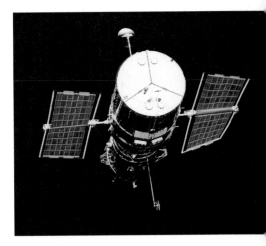

The solar arrays, attached to the sides of the Hubble Space Telescope, are silicon panels that use light from the sun to generate electrical power.

Space Flight Center in Huntsville, Alabama, and the Space Telescope Science Institute.

Reporters from newspapers and radio and television stations were there with the scientists to watch the first images from the new telescope. The press had carried many stories about the telescope during all the years it was being built. The public's expectations for the telescope were very high.[5]

Controllers at the Goddard Space Flight Center sent a set of commands to the telescope. Orbiting 375 miles above Earth, the telescope responded, turning slowly to catch the light from a star cluster thirteen hundred light-years away. It was the star cluster NGC 3532.

The light from the distant star cluster hit the primary mirror, bounced up to the smaller secondary mirror, and traveled back through the central opening in the primary mirror. The twice-reflected light then bounced off another mirror and into the WF/PC, which recorded the image. All was going according to plan.

The scientists who had gathered at the three centers knew the telescope had received its aiming commands. All of them waited anxiously through several minutes for the image to appear on their computer screens.[6]

The orbiting telescope then came into the range of a data relay satellite. The telescope sent its data to the satellite, and the satellite relayed them down to Earth. Computers at the Goddard Space Flight Center received the data and transformed them into a picture, which was seen by scientists, reporters, and engineers at the Space Telescope Science Institute as well.

A fuzzy group of stars appeared on the screen. People in the rooms grew excited as the camera team processed the image through a set of computer programs that slightly sharpened the picture.

"Look at that!" some of them shouted.

"It works! Hubble works!" said others.[7]

The press reported this first image from the Hubble Space Telescope as a great success. Astronomers and NASA officials told the reporters that they did not

After being released from the shuttle's payload bay, the Hubble Space Telescope sent data of its first image to anxious scientists at the Goddard Space Flight Center.

expect a sharp, clear picture from the telescope the first time it was used. NASA knew it would take days or even a few weeks to get all of the telescope's instruments adjusted properly.

But as NASA adjusted the telescope, those days went by with no improvement in the images. No matter what they tried, the images remained blurry.

Weeks passed. The press wanted to know why the telescope was not yet producing amazing pictures of stars and galaxies. NASA scientists tried everything they knew to sharpen the images, but nothing worked.

When the telescope looked at a star, the image it produced had a bright point in the center surrounded by a strange blurry halo. NASA then put the telescope through a test that moved the primary mirror through its entire range of focus—very much like twisting the focus ring on a camera. As the primary mirror was moved from one end of its focus range to the other, it never produced a sharp picture.

This test led NASA scientists to a terrible conclusion: There was a flaw in the telescope's primary mirror.

The primary mirror had started out as a one-ton piece of optical-quality glass. Over a period of three years, two hundred pounds of the glass were carefully ground and polished away, until its shape was considered perfect to reflect the light from space. But something had gone wrong.

There was no way to ignore the evidence coming

from Hubble. Scientists were stunned when they realized the problem was with the eight-foot primary mirror—the very heart of the telescope.

The primary mirror had been ground and polished incorrectly. It suffered from what astronomers called a spherical aberration. One edge of the mirror was ten-thousandths of an inch too flat, a measurement one-fiftieth the width of a human hair. This measurement is invisible to the human eye.[8]

No matter how small the flaw, the result was that the telescope's mirror could not focus light into a sharp point.

The Hubble Space Telescope, the most powerful telescope ever built, could not be focused.

The high hopes for the Hubble Space Telescope had been shattered. The entire project quickly became a huge source of embarrassment to NASA. The press harshly criticized them for the expensive failure. It was not long until the blurred space telescope became a source of jokes for comedians and cartoonists.

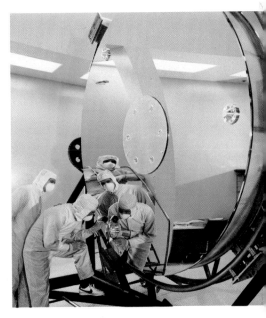

Prior to launch of the Hubble Telescope, technicians inspect the eight-foot primary mirror. As it turned out, the mirror had been ground and polished incorrectly.

What could be done to fix a broken telescope that had already cost NASA $1.6 billion to build and launch into space? Scientists could not simply climb into it and fix it. It was in space, in orbit around Earth. The first scheduled mission to service the telescope was not for another four years!

The flaw in the primary mirror was not the telescope's only problem. As the telescope orbited from the light to the dark sides of Earth, the heating and cooling of the solar arrays caused the telescope to wobble. The guidance system was also having problems pointing the telescope at the correct objects in space.

NASA scientists began thinking of ideas that might solve the telescope's many problems. Some at NASA wanted to capture the telescope with the shuttle and bring it back to Earth for repair. Others believed such a plan would not work. Once the telescope was back on the ground, they believed there would be no support from the public to repair it and get it back into space again.[9]

It was clear that a daring mission to repair the telescope in space would have to be planned.

NASA designed a complex repair mission and built special tools that scientists believed could be used to correct the focus of the primary mirror and fix the guidance system.

Only a repair in space could save the Hubble Space Telescope.

Hubble Trouble

As NASA discovered each new problem with the telescope, scientists worked hard at finding ways to solve it. If a problem could not be corrected from the ground, it became part of the planning for the repair mission. The solution to some of these problems involved designing and building new instruments that could be installed aboard the telescope. Installing these new instruments would be the work of a team of astronauts on NASA's first repair mission in space.

Detailed plans for the mission to repair the Hubble Space Telescope began in the summer of 1990. The long list of repairs took shape through 1991 and most of 1992. Because of the huge cost of these repairs, the stakes for the repair mission were high. NASA's reputation, and possibly its future, was on the line. Much would be gained by the mission's success, and much would be lost if it failed.

For the all-important mission, NASA selected one of the most experienced crews of astronauts it had ever assembled. Their training began more than a year before the mission, which was scheduled to launch in December 1993.

"I'm not overconfident," said astronaut Story Musgrave. "I'm running scared." Musgrave was the mission's payload commander, and he was responsible for coordinating the space walks that would repair the telescope. He knew how big a job the mission was going to be for him and the crew. "This thing is frightening to me. I'm looking for every kind of thing that might get out and bite us."[1]

Musgrave had been a surgeon before he came to NASA. When asked why he gave up surgery to become an astronaut, he quickly answered, "Why, so I could operate on the Hubble, of course."[2]

Dick Covey was the mission commander, in charge of the overall success and safety of the mission. Kenneth Bowersox, whom everyone called Sox, would back up Covey as shuttle pilot.

Mission specialist Claude Nicollier would operate the shuttle's robotic arm, or Remote Manipulator System (RMS). He would use the arm to grab and release the telescope. During the repairs, a fellow astronaut would

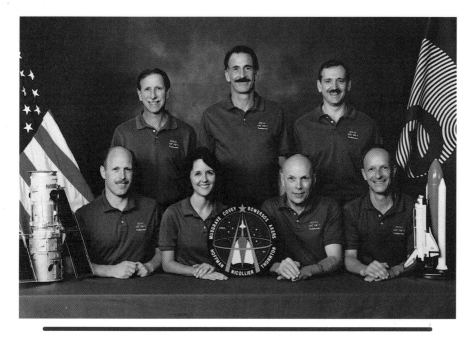

These seven astronauts were scheduled for the first Hubble Telescope servicing mission. Pictured are (front row, from left to right) Kenneth Bowersox, Kathryn Thornton, Story Musgrave, and Claude Nicollier; (back row) Richard Covey, Jeffrey Hoffman, and Thomas Akers.

be attached to the end of the arm. Nicollier would move the astronaut around the shuttle's payload bay in the same way a firefighter is moved when in the bucket of a cherry picker.

Two teams of spacewalkers would make the repairs to the telescope. Musgrave's spacewalking partner would be mission specialist Jeffrey Hoffman. The other spacewalking team would be mission specialists Thomas Akers and Kathryn "K.T." Thornton. All four had conducted space walks on previous missions.

After months of exhaustive training, the team of astronauts was ready for the daring mission. In the darkness at 1:00 A.M. on December 2, 1993, the crew rode to the launchpad at the Kennedy Space Center, Florida, and climbed aboard the space shuttle *Endeavour*. Strapped into their seats, they waited through the countdown as the launch drew nearer. Once again, everyone involved with the Hubble Space Telescope was watching.

Endeavour sat on the launchpad, lit up with spotlights. Only seconds to go.

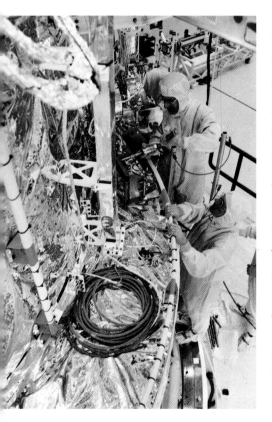

"Ten . . . nine . . . eight . . . seven . . . and GO for main engine start," said the public-address announcer. "Five . . . four . . . three . . . two . . . one." At 4:27 A.M., the shuttle's engines ignited, lighting up the night as it thundered off the pad into the early morning sky. "And we have liftoff . . . liftoff of the space shuttle *Endeavour*

Workers assemble one of the two solar panels on the Hubble Telescope. During the repair mission in space, one of the solar panels would need replacement.

and an ambitious mission to service the Hubble Space Telescope."[3]

In a matter of minutes, *Endeavour* and its crew were in orbit around Earth. They were now chasing the telescope. Over the next two days, *Endeavour* would gradually close the distance between them. The astronauts spent this period checking all the shuttle's systems and getting used to the sensation of weightlessness.

Early on the third day, *Endeavour*'s crew caught its first sight of the Hubble. Commander Dick Covey and pilot Ken Bowersox guided the shuttle gradually closer to the telescope.

"Now it's all eyeballs and hands," Bowersox said.[4] He knew the control thrusters of the shuttle had only enough fuel for one try at getting close enough to the telescope. They had to get it right.

Claude Nicollier took his place at the controls of the robotic arm. *Endeavour* drew closer and closer to the telescope. Nicollier reached out with the arm, and its claw gently grasped the Hubble Space Telescope.

Commander Covey said to Mission Control: "*Endeavour* has a firm handshake with Mr. Hubble's telescope."[5] Covey's announcement caused a sigh of relief in the Mission Control room. The telescope was in place in the shuttle's payload bay. The long and challenging task of repairing the telescope could begin.

The following day, Story Musgrave and Jeffrey

Hoffman helped each other slide into their cumbersome space suits for the repair mission's first space walk. Their task was to replace the telescope's faulty gyroscopes. Gyroscopes are instruments that are used to keep vehicles such as boats, airplanes, and spacecraft steady. The telescope needed the gyroscopes to keep it steady when scientists pointed it in the direction they wanted to look. Three of the telescope's six gyroscopes had failed and needed to be replaced.

Musgrave and Hoffman entered the airlock and closed the hatch behind them. The airlock is a room in which air pressure is slowly reduced to what the astronauts experience outside the protection of the shuttle. This had to occur before they opened the other hatch and floated out into space. The astronauts kept themselves attached to the payload bay by metal cables. Musgrave slowly made his way toward the telescope, which stood upright at the rear of the payload bay. Hoffman attached his feet to the end of the robotic arm. Nicollier then moved Hoffman and the arm toward the telescope.

Musgrave and Hoffman opened the panel doors near the bottom of the telescope. The two astronauts worked well together and had no problem replacing the gyroscope mechanisms. But when they were finished, Musgrave discovered he could not get the panel doors shut again. One of the doors was sagging.

They tried different tools to force the doors shut, but

Astronaut Story Musgrave is holding onto one of the handrails on the Hubble Space Telescope during the first of five space walks.

none worked. Musgrave suggested using something called a come-along. This tool had a crank that would pull the doors together and hold them. With the come-along holding the doors together, Musgrave used his hands to push them shut.[6]

The incident with the doors showed the astronauts that not everything was going to go perfectly. They would have to be clever and resourceful to overcome some of the mission's unexpected problems.

Musgrave and Hoffman's next task was to prepare the equipment for the removal of the solar arrays on either side of the telescope. The arrays were designed to roll up like window blinds. The first array rolled up perfectly. The other array had been warped. It would not roll up. The safest thing to do with the broken array was to throw it out into space, away from the shuttle. That job would be done the following day by Tom Akers and Kathy Thornton.

Akers and Thornton pulled on their space suits and went to work on the mission's second space walk. Thornton was at the end of the robotic arm. She steadied the solar array while Akers disconnected it. He had to be very careful not to bend the pins that held the electrical connectors. If they were bent, they could not be used to attach the new solar arrays. Without the solar arrays, the telescope would have no power.

Akers slowly and carefully disconnected each bolt and pin as the shuttle orbited into Earth's night side. Finally the solar array was free. Thornton alone held the solar array. She had to hold it perfectly still. If it began to move around, it could hit the telescope and damage it. While Thornton held the array, Nicollier used the robotic arm to move her and the array slowly away from the telescope.

"OK, Claude, real easy," she said.[7]

At that moment they were still on the night side of Earth. They needed to wait until daylight when the entire crew could see clearly, in case the solar array threatened to float back against the telescope when it was released. Thornton had to hold the solar array at the end of the robotic arm for several minutes, waiting for daylight. As *Endeavour* orbited onward, Thornton's partner finally saw light appear on Earth's horizon.

"I think I see sunrise coming, K.T.," Akers said.[8]

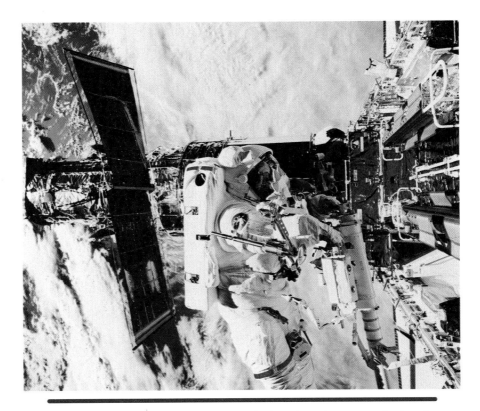

Astronaut Kathryn Thornton is attached to the robotic arm during the mission's second space walk.

Endeavour and its spacewalkers orbited into daylight.

"OK, Tom," Musgrave said from inside the shuttle. "Tell K.T. to go for release."

"OK, K.T. You ready?" Akers asked.

"Ready," Thornton said.

"Got a go for release," Akers said.[9]

At that moment Thornton released both her hands from the array. "OK. No hands," Thornton said. Bowersox immediately used *Endeavour*'s control thrusters to steer the shuttle away from the floating solar array. The crew watched as the solar array floated safely away from the shuttle.[10] The solar array would stay in orbit for some time before eventually burning up in Earth's atmosphere.

Thornton and Akers successfully attached the new solar arrays. They crawled back inside the shuttle for a well-deserved rest.

The third space walk was a big one. The task for Musgrave and Hoffman this time was to replace the Wide Field Planetary Camera, or WF/PC, with an improved version called WF/PC 2. This was probably the most delicate operation of the mission.

Hoffman held the large camera in his hands as he stood at the end of the robotic arm. He had to hold the camera very steady while Musgrave carefully removed the protective cover from the mirror. The mirror of the new camera was just several inches from the faceplate of Musgrave's helmet. If he touched or bumped the exposed mirror even slightly, the mirror would be knocked out of alignment—a disaster that would ruin the camera before it ever took its first picture.

Musgrave moved out of the way slowly and precisely. He then helped Hoffman guide WF/PC 2 snugly into its slot in the telescope. The camera was in place, and the third space walk was another success.

It was Akers and Thornton's turn again. Their task for the fourth space walk was to install a device that was of central importance to the telescope. It was called COSTAR, which stood for Corrective Optics Space Telescope Axial Replacement. This was the device that scientists had designed to correct the flaw in the telescope's primary mirror.

COSTAR was a metal box the size of a refrigerator. It contained a set of ten movable mirrors, each of which was no larger than a thumbnail.[11] Once COSTAR was installed in the telescope,

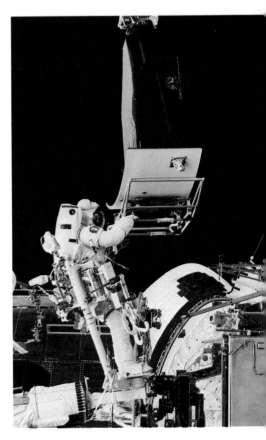

Jeffrey Hoffman carefully holds the Wide Field Planetary Camera during replacement operations.

it would deploy these mirrors. The mirrors would reflect the primary mirror's light in a way that would correct its flaw. In other words, although they could not correct the primary mirror itself, they could correct the path of light reflected from it.

Nicollier guided Thornton forward at the end of the robotic arm, where she held COSTAR in her hands. However, it was so big that she could not see where she was going. Akers served as her eyes. He hummed as he helped Thornton guide the mechanism into place. Nicollier was listening at the controls of the robotic arm.

"It was good to hear Tom humming," Nicollier said later, "because we knew when Tom was humming things were going well. And Tom was humming most of the time!"[12]

Akers and Thornton slid COSTAR into its tight fit inside the telescope. The major repairs of the mission were completed. They were almost home free.

On the fifth and final space walk there was a bit of drama. Musgrave and Hoffman were wrapping up the repairs when a small screw escaped from Musgrave's tool bag. If it was lost, there could be trouble. The space shuttle is a very complex machine. Even something as small as a loose screw floating inside the shuttle's payload bay during reentry could spell disaster.

They had to catch the screw. Musgrave was attached to the end of the robotic arm, and Hoffman was tethered to it. But the screw was floating down and away from

Attached to the end of the white robotic arm, Kathryn Thornton prepares to install the refrigerator-sized COSTAR. Thomas Akers assists from inside the bay.

them into the payload bay, where it would become impossible to find. Nicollier saw the screw's glinting light from his place at the robotic arm's controls. He quickly began to guide Hoffman and Musgrave down in its direction. Nicollier was moving the arm much faster than usual, because he knew it was very important to capture the tumbling screw.

Hoffman reached out his hand as they chased it. Down and down toward the payload bay they went.

Just as Hoffman's feet were about to bump into the side of the payload bay, he caught it. "I have it," he said.

"Okay, arm stop," Musgrave said quickly.[13]

The screw was returned to the bag. With a sigh of relief, Musgrave and Hoffman went about their work and completed the repairs.

On the following day, the newly repaired Hubble Space Telescope was released back into orbit. The crew of *Endeavour* had done their best on the telescope. They had conducted five space walks—more space walks than any other U.S. astronauts or Russian cosmonauts had ever conducted on any single mission. It was an impressive record. After eleven successful days in space, they were ready to come home.

Endeavour made a night landing at the Kennedy Space Center in Florida. As far as the astronauts knew, nothing had gone wrong on their mission. But they did not yet know if their mission had been a success.

NASA scientists and astronomers around the world once again focused their attention on the Hubble Space Telescope. All waited to see if the repairs had worked.

3

Hubble's Second Chance

A few days after *Endeavour*'s astronauts had returned to Earth, a group of scientists and astronomers gathered at the Space Telescope Science Institute. Although the *Endeavour* mission had appeared to be flawless, no one would know for sure if the repairs were successful until the telescope was fully tested. It was the first day of those important tests, the day the telescope would produce its first images from the new WF/PC 2.

The new corrective optics were delicately deployed inside the telescope. Scientists at the institute waited anxiously as power was fed to the telescope's other controls and instruments.[1] Everything looked good as it moved through a series of checkout commands. The new gyroscopes reacted as the telescope was pointed at a distant star called AGK +81 D226.[2]

Again the telescope recorded the image in its computers. Minutes passed as the telescope's orbit carried it around Earth and into the range of the relay satellite.

Scientists in the control room watched their monitor. Light surged through the screen. There was a momentary flicker before the image steadied.

A silence fell over the room as the image from space appeared. There on the screen was the clear, sharp picture of their targeted star!

Cheers and applause erupted throughout the room. Scientists shook hands and slapped each other's backs. The new picture was fantastic. The repaired telescope was working beyond their wildest expectations. It was a joyous moment for them all.[3]

The new instruments skillfully installed during the daring repair mission were tremendously successful. The Hubble Space Telescope was finally able to photograph distant objects in space with a clarity ten times greater than the most powerful telescopes on Earth.

Work with the Hubble Space Telescope was only beginning.

In February 1997 another team of astronauts was sent into space to make further improvements to the telescope. Ken Bowersox, who had been the shuttle pilot on the repair mission in 1993, was the commander on

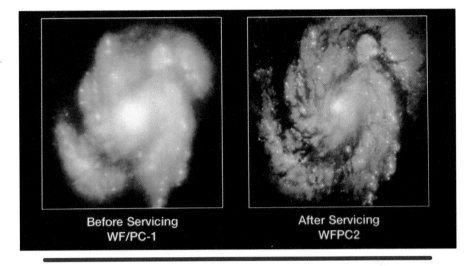

Before Servicing
WF/PC-1

After Servicing
WFPC2

The dramatic improvement in the image seen from Hubble, shown on the right, could not have been accomplished without the repair mission.

this mission aboard the space shuttle *Discovery*. Bowersox and his crew removed the Faint-Object Spectrograph and installed the Near-Infrared Camera and Multi-Object Spectrometer, or NICMOS. NICMOS photographs and measures the infrared wavelengths of light from objects in the universe. Infrared wavelengths cannot be detected by the human eye.

The 1997 *Discovery* mission also installed the Space Telescope Imaging Spectrograph to make more sensitive studies of ultraviolet light from objects in space. The astronauts also replaced one of the three guidance sensors and a number of other components aboard the telescope.

The 1993 repair mission and the 1997 servicing mission have put the Hubble Space Telescope in excellent working condition. With the telescope's continuing use by astronomers—and more improvements planned for the future—it may help us answer some of our most important questions about the universe.

The Hubble Space Telescope is sometimes described as both a telescope and a time machine. This is because the telescope may be able to tell us how old the universe is.

How?

Astronomers measure the vast distances in our universe by light-years. A light-year is the distance light will travel through space in one year. Light travels at the incredible speed of 186,000 miles per second. Light, moving at that speed, will travel 5.9 trillion miles in a year. One light-year, then, equals 5.9 trillion miles.

Our own solar system lies 25,000 light-years from the center of our Milky Way galaxy. That seems like a very great distance in space. But the Hubble Space Telescope, after its repairs in 1993, is able to see 13 billion light-years away!

The important thing to remember is this: The light reaching us from that distance has been traveling 13 billion years. The telescope's picture of a galaxy 13 billion light-years away is not a picture of how that galaxy appears now. It is a picture of how that galaxy appeared 13 billion years ago, when those light rays began their journey to us.

In this way, the Hubble Space Telescope serves as a time machine. The greater the distance the telescope sees into space, the farther it sees into the past. It may one day be able to see almost to the beginning of the universe. Such discoveries may help astronomers learn how the universe was formed.

The Hubble Space Telescope is an amazing tool for

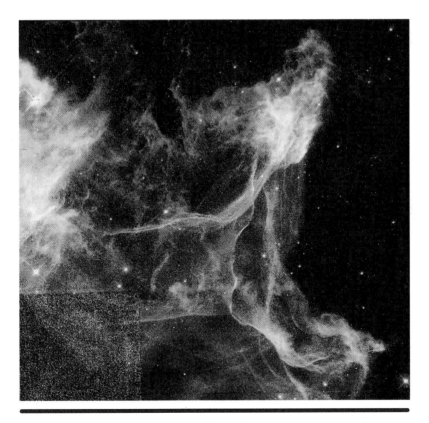

The colorful blast wave from this supernova explosion occurred 15,000 years ago.

astronomers. Astronaut Story Musgrave, who risked his life in the daring space walks to repair the Hubble, understood that the telescope may answer questions about the universe that are important to us all.

"It is a reach out there for the heavens," he said, "to find out what this universe is all about."[4]

4

Eye on the Universe

The Hubble Space Telescope is not only a new and powerful eye on distant objects in space. The information and pictures that have streamed down from Hubble since 1990 have proven that it is also a window through which we can see the past and future of our universe.

In 1987, three years before Hubble was launched, astronomers observed the explosion of a star 169,000 light-years away. The death or explosion of a star is called a supernova. Astronomers named this one Supernova 1987A.

In February 1994, the Hubble Space Telescope took pictures of the seven-year-old supernova. The fascinating images showed an expanding ring of gas around the

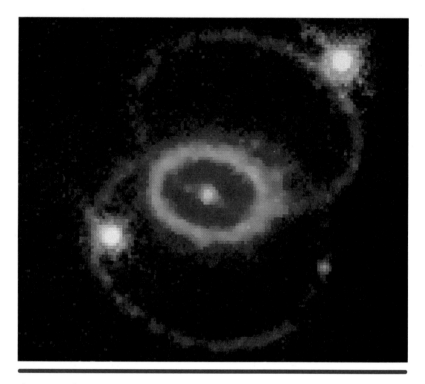

A pair of mysterious rings of glowing gas surround the site of this exploded star that astronomers call Supernova 1987A.

dying star, plus two other rings that seemed to intersect each other.

"The Hubble images of the rings are quite spectacular and unexpected," said Dr. Chris Burrows of the Space Telescope Science Institute.[1] Burrows believes the inner ring is on the same plane of view as the supernova, but that the other two rings are behind and in front of it. The two outer rings, according to Burrows, could be jets of material from an unseen source, such as another star or black hole very close to the supernova. Burrows believes the rings were lit up when they were hit by waves of radiation from the exploding star.[2]

Seeing out into the mind-boggling reaches of distant galaxies is not the only way that Hubble aids astronomers. Closer to home, the Hubble Space Telescope has observed a number of remarkable things in our own solar system. Hubble has given us our first view of the surface of our most distant planet, Pluto. It has detected a thin atmosphere of oxygen around one of Jupiter's larger moons, Europa. The telescope also recorded images of a rare storm on the ringed planet Saturn. The giant storm shown by the telescope on Saturn in December 1994 was larger than the entire Earth.

The Hubble Space Telescope took an incredible series of pictures in July 1994, as fragments of the Shoemaker-Levy 9 comet bombarded the planet Jupiter.

A rare storm on the planet Saturn, visible near the equator, was recorded by the Hubble Telescope.

Chunks of the Shoemaker-Levy 9 comet, shown here, collided with Jupiter in 1994.

Over a period of six days, astronomers watched the dramatic pictures beamed down from Hubble. The spectacular images showed gigantic fireball explosions as the comet fragments entered Jupiter's atmosphere. As the planet rotated, the telescope recorded the giant dark splotches blown into Jupiter's atmosphere by the exploding fragments. Some of the splotches were as large as four thousand miles across.

In January 1995, the telescope took striking pictures of the planetary nebula NGC 6543. A nebula is a giant cloud of gas in space, often surrounding a dying star, such as the one in NGC 6543. What is so striking about Hubble's images from this dying star is the expanding gas shells and the symmetrical structure of the gaseous rings.

Astronomer Patrick Harrington of the University of Maryland studied the nebula images and related them to the future of our own sun: "Because this [image] represents the last stages in the evolution of ordinary stars, a star like our sun is going to go through an episode of this sort, maybe five or six billion years from now. So, in some sense, when we look at an object like this, we are looking at the future of our own solar system."[3]

The telescope also aided NASA in predicting the weather on Mars when the *Pathfinder* spacecraft prepared for its landing on the planet in July 1997. In the days before the scheduled landing, images from Hubble showed giant dust storms heading toward the area where *Pathfinder* would land. These pictures alerted scientists involved with the landing mission to prepare for dusty conditions that might threaten the success of *Pathfinder*.

Then, shortly before the spacecraft's scheduled landing on July 4, the telescope showed NASA that the potentially troubling dust storms had died down. Everything looked okay again to go ahead with the landing. The amazing telescope, orbiting Earth, had proved very useful in giving NASA an up-to-date weather forecast from Mars.

Also in July 1997, the telescope helped discover the most distant galaxy ever found in the universe to date. The detailed image showed a

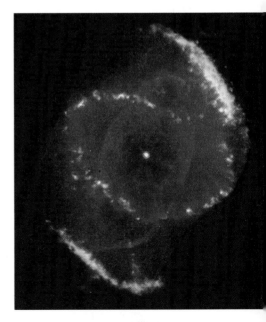

Planetary nebula NGC 6543 is also known as the cat's eye nebula.

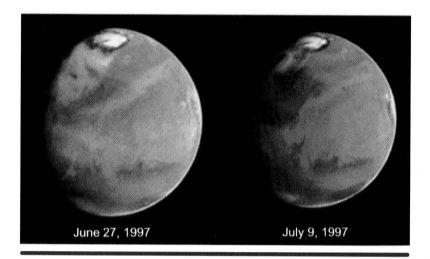

June 27, 1997   July 9, 1997

The image of Mars on the left shows the dust storms that threatened the landing of Pathfinder. *On the right, the wispy clouds are gone and the* Pathfinder *landing is no longer in danger.*

young galaxy 13 billion light-years away. In August of the same year, the Hubble Telescope recorded what may be the first image of a planet that exists outside of our solar system.[4]

In the years since its launch, Hubble has helped astronomers come close to answering many questions about our universe. The telescope has gotten us closer to the answers only because thousands of astronomers, engineers, and other scientists insisted that these answers be pursued.

From the scientists who built the telescope to the astronauts who repaired it, all believed the quest for knowledge about the universe was worth the tremendous efforts and risks. Despite many difficulties, setbacks, and failures, the people involved with the Hubble Space Telescope have pressed ahead to a future made brighter with the light of knowledge. Sandra Faber, an astronomer with the telescope's Wide Field Planetary Camera team, summed it up best. "The Hubble Space Telescope is just as complex as the people who made it," she said. "Like them, it has the potential to be heroic. It is proving that now."[5]

Heroic efforts of human curiosity produced the Hubble Space Telescope—our clearer, sharper eye on the universe.

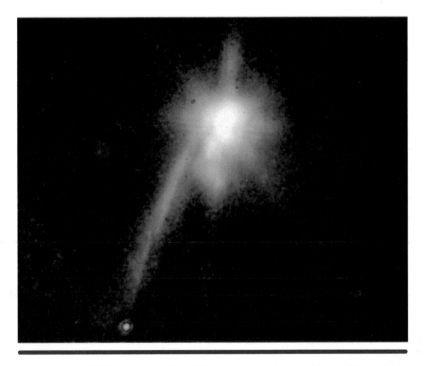

In August 1997, the Hubble Telescope revealed a long, thin nebula pointing to a faint object (bottom left). This object, named TMR-1C, may be the first planet outside our solar system to ever be recorded.

CHAPTER NOTES

Chapter 1. A Telescope Bound for Space

1. Carolyn Collins Petersen and John C. Brandt, *Hubble Vision: Astronomy with the Hubble Space Telescope* (New York: Cambridge University Press, 1995), p. 33.

2. Elaine Scott and Margaret Miller, *Adventure in Space: The Flight to Fix the Hubble* (New York: Hyperion Books for Children, 1995), p. 10.

3. Robert W. Smith, *The Space Telescope: A Study of NASA, Science, Technology, and Politics* (New York: Cambridge University Press, 1989), pp. 245–246, 253–256.

4. Petersen and Brandt, p. 68.

5. Ibid., p. 3.

6. Ibid., pp. 2–3.

7. Ibid., pp. 3–5.

8. Jay Barbree and Martin Caidin, *A Journey Through Time: Exploring the Universe with the Hubble Space Telescope* (New York: Penguin Books, 1995), p. xii.

9. *Rescue Mission in Space: The Hubble Space Telescope*, NOVA Adventures in Science, 1994 (video).

Chapter 2. Hubble Trouble

1. Elaine Scott, *Adventure in Space: The Flight to Fix the Hubble* (New York: Hyperion Books for Children, 1995), p. 5.

2. Ibid., p. 13.

3. *Rescue Mission in Space: The Hubble Space Telescope*, NOVA Adventures in Science, 1994 (video).

4. Scott, p. 48.

5. NOVA video.

6. Scott, p. 51.

7. Ibid., pp. 52–53.

8. Ibid., p. 53.

9. Ibid.

10. NOVA video.

11. Jay Barbree and Martin Caidin, *A Journey Through Time: Exploring the Universe with the Hubble Space Telescope* (New York: Penguin Books, 1995), p. xiv.

12. Scott, p. 55.

13. NOVA video.

Chapter 3. Hubble's Second Chance

1. Carolyn Collins Petersen and John C. Brandt, *Hubble Vision: Astronomy with the Hubble Space Telescope* (New York: Cambridge University Press, 1995), pp. 43–44.

2. Jay Barbree and Martin Caidin, *A Journey Through Time: Exploring the Universe with the Hubble Space Telescope* (New York: Penguin Books, 1995), p. xix.

3. Ibid.

4. *Rescue Mission in Space: The Hubble Space Telescope*, NOVA Adventures in Science, 1994 (video).

Chapter 4. Eye on the Universe

1. Space Telescope Science Institute, "Hubble Finds Mysterious Ring Structure Around Supernova 1987A," *Hubble Space Telescope News*, press release No. STScI-PR94-22, May 19, 1994.

2. Carolyn Collins Petersen and John C. Brandt, *Hubble Vision: Astronomy with the Hubble Space Telescope* (New York: Cambridge University Press, 1995), p. 160.

3. Space Telescope Science Institute, *Hubble Space Telescope News*, transcript of video accompanying photo release STScI-PRC95-01, January 11, 1995.

4. Malcolm W. Browne, "Image Is Believed to Be the First of a Planet Beyond Solar System," *The New York Times*, May 29, 1998, p. A1.

5. Petersen and Brandt, p. 233.

GLOSSARY

COSTAR—Corrective Optics Space Telescope Axial Replacement. The instrument placed inside the Hubble Space Telescope to correct the flaw in the telescope's primary mirror.

deploy—To move an object, such as a satellite, into position.

Faint-Object Camera—Unique camera aboard the Hubble Space Telescope that takes pictures of exceptionally faint objects too dim to be seen by telescopes on Earth. It was developed by the European Space Agency, an important contributor to the telescope project.

Goddard High-Resolution Spectrograph—Instrument aboard the Hubble Space Telescope that analyzes ultraviolet light from glowing objects in space.

guidance system—The system aboard the Hubble Space Telescope that points it in the direction scientists wish to view.

gyroscope—A spinning device used to stabilize vehicles such as boats, planes, or spacecraft. They are an important part of the Hubble Space Telescope's guidance system.

High-Speed Photometer—Instrument aboard the Hubble Space Telescope that can measure the size or magnitude of a star and its distance from Earth.

light-year—A measure of distance used by astronomers. Light travels at 186,000 miles per second, covering a distance of 5.9 trillion miles in one year. Therefore, 5.9 trillion miles equals one light-year.

optical telescope assembly—The central component of the Hubble Space Telescope, consisting of the primary and secondary mirror construction.

payload bay—The area of the space shuttle where cargo is stored.

Remote Manipulator System—The robotic arm in the payload bay of the space shuttle. It is controlled from the rear of the shuttle's flight deck and was a major tool in the repair of the Hubble Space Telescope.

solar array—Silicon panels that use light from the sun to generate electrical power. The Hubble Space Telescope is powered by two solar arrays attached to either side of the telescope.

spectrograph—An instrument that divides light rays or other forms of radiation into a spectrum and then records that spectrum.

spherical aberration—Defect in the curvature of an optical mirror, preventing light from being focused into a single point. The Hubble Space Telescope's primary mirror had this type of flaw.

ultraviolet—A part of the light spectrum that is invisible to human eyes. Most ultraviolet light from space is absorbed by Earth's atmosphere.

Wide Field Planetary Camera—Camera aboard the Hubble Space Telescope that takes pictures of wider areas of the sky than the Faint-Object Camera. It can also narrow its field of vision to take detailed pictures of nearby objects such as planets, asteroids, and comets.

FURTHER READING

Books

Lampton, Christopher. *The Space Telescope*. New York: Franklin Watts, 1987.

Mitton, Jacqueline, and Stephen P. Maran. *Gems of Hubble*. New York: Cambridge University Press, 1996.

Petersen, Carolyn Collins, and John C. Brandt. *Hubble Vision: Astronomy with the Hubble Space Telescope*. New York: Cambridge University Press, 1995.

Scott, Elaine, and Margaret Miller. *Adventure in Space: The Flight to Fix the Hubble*. New York: Hyperion Books for Children, 1995.

Scott, Elaine. *Close Encounters: What Hubble Saw*. New York: Disney Press, 1998.

Sipiera, Paul P., and Diane M. Sipiera. *The Hubble Space Telescope*. Chicago, Ill.: Children's Press, 1997.

Internet Sources

Association of Universities for Research in Astronomy. "Hubble." *Space Telescope Science Institute*. 1996. <http://www.stsci.edu/> (June 26, 1998).

California Institute of Technology. "Hubble." *Welcome to the Planets$^{(TM)}$ Home Page*. n.d. <http://pds.jpl.nasa.gov/planets/welcome/hubble.htm>(June 28, 1998).

NCC World Wide Web Services. *Hubble Space Telescope Information*. July 28, 1997. <http://www. ncc.com/misc/hubble_sites.html> (June 26, 1998).

INDEX